D1358672

2/05   DISCARDED

R.T. JONES MEMORIAL LIBRARY
CHILDREN'S DEPARTMENT
CANTON, GEORGIA 30114

SEQUOYAH REGIONAL LIBRARY

3 8749 0052 1829 6

21st Century Issues

ANIMAL RIGHTS

Kay Woodward

PROPERTY OF
THE SEQUOYAH REGIONAL
LIBRARY SYSTEM CANTON, GA.

WORLD ALMANAC® LIBRARY

Please visit our web site at: www.worldalmaclibrary.com
For a free color catalog describing World Almanac® Library's list of high-quality books and multimedia programs, call 1-800-848-2928 (USA) or 1-800-387-3178 (Canada). World Almanac® Library's fax: (414) 332-3567.

Library of Congress Cataloging-in-Publication Data

Woodward, Kay.
    Animal rights / by Kay Woodward.
      p. cm. — (21st century issues)
    Includes bibliographical references and index.
    ISBN 0-8368-5642-2 (lib. bdg.)
    ISBN 0-8368-5659-7 (softcover)
    1. Animal rights—Juvenile literature. 2. Animal welfare—Juvenile literature.
  HV4708.W66   2004
  179'.3—dc22   2004043387

This North American edition first published in 2005 by
World Almanac® Library
330 West Olive Street, Suite 100
Milwaukee, WI 53212 USA

This U.S. edition copyright © 2005 by World Almanac® Library. Original edition copyright © 2004 by Arcturus Publishing Limited.

Series concept: Alex Woolf
Project editor: Kelly Davis
Designer: Paul Turner, Stonecastle Graphics
Consultant: Kaye Stearman
Picture researcher: Shelley Noronha, Glass Onion Pictures
World Almanac® Library editor: Carol Ryback
World Almanac® Library designer: Kami Koenig

Photo credits:
Popperfoto: Regis Duvignau 8; Russell Boyce 10; Anthony P. Bolante 23; Peter Macdiarmid 24; Enny Nuraheni 30; Will Burgess 32, 33; Claudia Daut 38; Duncan Willetts 41; Hyungwon Kang 44. RSPCA: Tom Claxton 6; Dr. Matt Ruglys 11; Colin Seddon 12; Robin Culley 29, 31. Niva G. Images: title page, 36. RSPCA/Angela Hampton 7, 28. Rex Features: cover, 19. Science Photo Library: 20, 26. Topham: Nancy Richmond 5; EMPICS, 14, 16, 17; Fritz Hoffmann 21; John Griffin 25; The British Library 34; David Jamieson/PAL 37; David Jennings 39; Charles Walker 40; Polfoto 42, 43.

All rights reserved. No part of this book may be reproduced, stored in a retrieval system, or transmitted in any form or by any means, electronic, mechanical, photocopying, recording, or otherwise, without the prior written permission of the copyright holder.

Printed in Italy

1 2 3 4 5 6 7 8 9 08 07 06 05 04

Cover: Protesters at an animal rights demonstration in Helsinki, Finland, cage themselves to raise awareness of the suffering of animals on fur farms.

CONTENTS

1: WHAT ARE ANIMAL RIGHTS?

Do animals deserve to be treated with the same respect as humans? As long as the animals do not suffer, should humans be allowed to use them in experiments? Is it ethical to allow the hunting of certain animals? Does a dolphin have more right to live than an insect? What exactly are animal rights?

Humans and animals

There is no simple definition of "animal rights" because people of various countries and cultures view animals differently. Some people believe that animals have exactly the same rights as humans. These people feel that animals have the right to be free and should not be used in farming, owned as pets, or subjected to medical experiments. The view that humans are no more important than animals is often considered extreme.

Other people believe that humans have the right to use animals in farming, keep them as pets, and experiment on them as long as they are cared for, treated with respect, and protected from unnecessary pain. This attitude is often called believing in animal welfare.

The animal rights movement

Although concerns about the welfare of animals were first voiced in nineteenth-century England, it was not until 1975, when philosophers such as Peter Singer, Richard Ryder, and Tom Regan began to raise questions about animals' rights,

Perspectives

The FAWC (Farm Animal Welfare Council) in the United Kingdom lists the "Five Freedoms" below as guidelines for acceptable animal welfare. These freedoms provide a definition of the basic rights many people believe animals should have:

1. Freedom from hunger and thirst.
2. Freedom from discomfort.
3. Freedom from pain, injury, or disease.
4. Freedom to behave normally.
5. Freedom from fear and distress.

Australian philosopher Peter Singer's 1975 book, *Animal Liberation,* contained many statements that helped launch the animal rights movement:

"Speciesism . . . is a prejudice . . . in favor of the interests of members of one's own species and against those of members of another species. It should be obvious that the fundamental objections to racism and sexism . . . apply equally to speciesism. If possessing a higher degree of intelligence does not entitle one human to use another for his or her own ends, how can it entitle humans to exploit nonhumans . . . ?"

that the animal rights movement gained momentum. Singer argued that although we view animals as less intelligent than ourselves, we have no right to exploit them. Ryder developed the concept of speciesism (discrimination against other species), which he compared to sexism and racism.

Since the 1970s, countless opinions from around the world have kept animal rights a very hotly debated topic.

Sheep from a ranch near Durango, Colorado, are herded on a three-day journey from their winter home to their spring home. Animal rights activists believe that sheep have the right to freedom from hunger, thirst, pain, discomfort, and fear.

Debate

Should animals and humans have the same rights?

2: FARMING

Farm animals are bred and reared in order to provide humans with products such as meat, eggs, milk, butter, cheese, and leather. Cattle, poultry, sheep, pigs, goats, horses, donkeys, mules, buffalo, oxen, and camels are just some of the animals that are used on farms around the world.

Some animal rights' groups protest because farm animals usually have a shorter life span than they would naturally enjoy. Other groups see farm animals' welfare as the biggest concern and work to ensure that farm animals are well treated.

Broilers and laying hens

Chicken farms are often the target of much negative publicity from animal rights' groups. The birds on these farms are bred for two purposes. Broilers are chickens of either sex that are bred just for their meat. Laying hens are female chickens that are bred to produce eggs for human consumption.

Most broilers spend their short lives in large barns with no access to the outdoor world. While their ancestors' life span lasted seven to nine years, broilers are slaughtered when they are only about six weeks old. (A carefully balanced diet containing protein, minerals, vitamins, and antibiotics makes the birds grow to adult size at a faster than natural rate.)

Some poultry barns on large factory farms keep chickens in long rows of cramped cages called batteries. Many hens are often crowded together in one cage. Europe plans to ban battery cages by 2012.

Laying hens each produce about three hundred eggs yearly. In Europe, they are killed for meat at twelve to eighteen months, because they start to lay fewer eggs after this time. More than 90 percent of laying hens are kept in cramped "battery" cages. These cages are so small that the birds cannot even flap their wings. The wire floors of the cages also cause many birds to develop foot problems. In the United States, some laying hens live for up to thirty-two months, but the majority of all hens still spend their time in battery cages.

Animal welfare groups have long campaigned for improved conditions for farmed chickens. Their efforts have led to better living conditions for a small percentage of broilers and laying hens. Free-range broilers and laying hens have access to the outdoors and plenty of space in which to roam. Organic broilers roam freely and eat whatever they find but are also fed organic food.

Free-range chickens and their eggs are labeled so that consumers know the birds were raised and handled in a humane manner. Many people believe that free-range meats and organic foods taste better. Labels such as "farm fresh" simply mean that the eggs came from farms; they were probably laid by hens in battery cages. Processed foods and baked goods are usually made with battery eggs—although some major supermarkets and restaurant chains now pledge that all eggs in their prepared meals are laid by free-range hens.

Free-range chickens spend their days roaming in fields.

Cattle

There are two types of cattle—dairy and beef. A typical dairy cow produces more than 6 gallons (23 liters) of milk a day. Cow's milk is used to make other dairy products, such as cream, cheese, and yogurt. Each dairy cow must give birth to one calf a year in order to keep producing milk. The calves are raised to adulthood as either dairy or beef cattle, or are kept from moving around and slaughtered when very young for their tender meat, called veal. Although the natural life span for most cattle is twenty to thirty years, dairy cows become worn out from producing so many offspring and so much milk, and are often slaughtered for their meat at about age five.

Beef cattle are bred just for their meat, which sells as steaks, chop meat, and sausages. Beef cattle roam outdoors for part of their lives and are slaughtered at about eighteen months, when the meat is at its best.

Some countries allow female cattle total freedom. In India, religious customs dictate a great respect for cows, and the animals roam freely, even in cities. Hinduism strictly forbids the slaughter of milk-producing cows for their meat.

Pâté de foie gras and veal

Sometimes meat eaters refuse to eat certain types of meat on the grounds that the animals are treated in a totally unacceptable way. The production of *pâté de foie gras* and veal raises the most controversy.

Pâté de foie gras is a smooth, rich paste made from the liver of a goose or duck that has been fattened by force-feeding. These birds are kept in small cages and overfed until their liver becomes ten times its normal size, which causes problems with breathing and walking. France produces and consumes about 90 percent of the foie gras in the world. Countries that ban production of foie gras may still import it. Animal rights activists are working for a total ban of foie gras.

A chef works near trays holding the traditional French delicacy, *pâté de foie gras*, made from livers. Ducks and geese are force-fed corn for more than a month to produce the livers, which weigh 18 to 21 ounces (500 to 600 grams).

Veal is the low-fat, pale meat of very young dairy calves. Calves raised for veal spend their entire lives in small enclosures that prevent them from moving around (exercise develops their muscles and darkens the meat). They are fed a special diet of milk and high-protein calf meal before being slaughtered as little as three weeks after their birth. The United Kingdom has banned the use of "veal crates" for calves. Animal-rights activists hope to stop this practice in other countries as well.

Intensive farming

Factory farms are designed to raise a large number of animals in a very small space for as much profit as possible. These enormous, largely automated enterprises have driven millions of small family farms out of business since 1945. The United States has lost about three million farms in the last sixty years.

Some agricultural experts claim that intensive farming methods (particularly including ground-up carcasses in animal feed) can help spread diseases, such as foot-and-mouth disease. In some cases, these diseases also spread to humans. Bovine spongiform encephalopathy (BSE), also known as "mad cow disease," has been linked with Creutzfeldt-Jakob disease (CJD) in humans. Both BSE and CJD cause brain abnormalities that are fatal to animals and humans. Organic farming—a return to natural animal breeding and raising crops without the use of chemicals—is becoming increasingly widespread. Organically produced meat is usually more expensive, but consumers can be confident that the animals were bred and raised in a more natural way. Organic farming of fruits and vegetables is also less cost effective, so consumers must expect higher prices.

 Perspectives

The Organic Farming Research Foundation in Santa Cruz, California, is optimistic about the future of organic farming:

"As the public becomes increasingly concerned about the negative effects of industrial agriculture on the environment and on their bodies, the demand for safe food is skyrocketing. Organic agriculture offers a bright light in the troubled future of family farming."

The Organic Farming Research Foundation web site, June 2003 (www.ofrf.org)

Animal transportation

Regulations regarding the type of animal being transported and the method of transportation vary widely for food animals. Livestock and poultry bound for slaughter may travel great distances by rail, barge, or truck. In 1873, the United States passed the "Twenty-Eight Hour Law," a federal law limiting the amount of time that animals being transported by rail or barge over state lines could go without food or water. That time limit was increased to thirty-six hours in 1994, except for poultry. The law does not apply to intrastate live food-animal shipments, and only four states—Rhode Island, Wisconsin, Pennsylvania, and Connecticut—regulate poultry shipments. Britain and other European countries employ much stricter control. In fact, Britain limits animal transport time without food and water to fifteen hours. Activists hope to reduce this time even further.

One of the most controversial issues is the way in which animals are moved to new farms or sent to slaughter. Federal law limits livestock transport times by truck or rail, but not via water or air, and U.S. poultry shipments have no restrictions. Truck transport of U.S. farm animals was not common until well into the twentieth century. Transportation of European livestock, such as sheep, is more strictly regulated than in the U.S.

Fishing

Since prehistoric times, humans have fished for food. Until recent centuries, however, the amount of fishing carried out in the oceans, rivers, and lakes of the world was not large enough to have a negative impact on the numbers and species of ocean creatures available for harvesting. Near the end of the 1800s, the fishing industry switched from sailing boats to motorized vessels. Further technological advances in ship design and ocean farming techniques in the twentieth century led to a huge increase in the numbers and types of fish caught. Refrigerated ships allow fishing vessels to process and store their catch as they travel around the globe for weeks or months.

Marine mammals, such as this harbor porpoise (also known as a common porpoise), must swim to the ocean surface to breathe. They often become tangled and suffer an agonizing death as they drown in fishing nets.

In the past, many people believed that—unlike humans and animals—fish did not feel pain (which is why some vegetarians eat fish, but not meat). In 2003, the results of experiments on trout suggested that fish do feel pain after all. This may affect future maritime laws regarding the catching and killing of fish.

Case Study

Overfishing and a decrease in both water quality and habitat are factors that have led to the decline of wild salmon around the world. As demand for salmon increases, suppliers turn to fish farms, which leads to concerns about how the animals are treated.

In 2002, Loch Duart in Scotland became the first fish farm to receive the Royal Society for the Prevention of Cruelty to Animals (RSPCA) Freedom Food certification for farmed salmon. Loch Duart provides its fish with a safe and healthy habitat that has no adverse impact on the environment. A fish welfare officer monitors the salmon to ensure that they have adequately sized areas in which to swim and that their feeding is controlled. There are also strict limits on the number of times the salmon are handled.

Managing Director Nick Joy says, "We have always regarded the welfare of our fish as extremely important. It also means that our customers receive a better tasting, better looking fish."

Sales Director Andrew Bing adds, "For our customers, Freedom Food is a label that means caring and responsible farming. To consumers who care about the quality of life of farmed animals, this is an important endorsement."

Offshore cages form a salmon farm in the Shetland Islands.

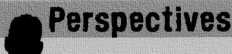

Perspectives

The Vegetarian Society promotes vegetarianism:

"The Vegetarian Society defines a vegetarian as a person who eats no meat, poultry, game, fish, shellfish, or crustacea. Vegetarians also avoid the by-products of slaughter such as gelatin or animal rennet in cheese. The Society only approves products containing eggs when they are free-range. . . . Vegetarianism is growing and becoming more mainstream, but vegetarians are still only a small proportion of the . . . population."

(www.navs-online.org)

Drift nets are large fishing nets with weights at the bottom and floats at the top, enabling them to drift through the ocean, catching fish such as tuna as they go. Unfortunately, drift nets also catch other marine creatures, such as dolphins, sea turtles, and sharks. Although the International Dolphin Conservation Act of 1992 called for the end of large-scale drift-net fishing, several countries still use this method. Animal rights and welfare organizations seek to end this practice.

Vegetarianism

A vegetarian is someone who eats no meat. About a quarter of the world's population lives on a mainly vegetarian diet, for moral, religious, or health reasons. In Europe and the United States, the proportion is much smaller, although vegetarian groups claim that more people are opting for a meat-free diet. Others extend or limit the range of food they eat, leading to different types of vegetarianism.

- Vegetarians do not eat meat, fish, or poultry.
- Piscatarians do not eat meat, but will eat fish and seafood.
- Vegans do not eat or use any animal products. They also refuse to use products and clothing, such as furniture and leather shoes, that are made from animals.

Debate

There are many arguments regarding whether or not the farming of animals is carried out in a humane or inhumane way. If the whole world were to turn into vegetarians, what would become of farm animals? Where would they live? Could they survive in the wild? Who would feed them if they couldn't find food on their own?

3: HUNTING

Chasing and killing wild animals ("game") is known as hunting. There are three main types of hunting—hunting for sport, hunting for food, and hunting to control animal numbers. People often hunt for more than one of these reasons. Those who take part in these activities feel that their actions are justifiable, but many animal lovers feel strongly that hunting should be banned altogether.

The history of hunting

In the past, people hunted in order to survive. After an animal was killed, nothing was wasted. Its meat was eaten, its skin made into clothing, its bones formed into tools. In time, people increasingly turned their attention toward agriculture, which provided other sources of food. Wild animals were still hunted, but people also raised livestock and grew crops to eat.

This drawing depicts a medieval stag hunt with hounds.

Perspectives

Founded in 1957, Friends of Animals is a U.S.-based activist group that works to protect animals from cruelty and abuse:

"Friends of Animals opposes hunting: All hunting. The more we study the excuses offered by hunters, the more we see they are baseless. Friends of Animals holds that hunting is ethically wrong—it imposes capital punishment on innocent animals essentially for the amusement or 'recreation' of someone who enjoys killing. Friends of Animals has determined that hunting is ecologically disruptive, and...considers hunting to be sociologically disreputable."

(www.friendsofanimals.org)

Around the seventh century B.C., rulers and nobles began hunting for sport. The idea of keeping game, such as deer or pheasants, in order to hunt them was firmly established by the seventeenth century, when hunting was linked with owning land. By that time, many hunters used guns in order to more easily kill their quarry from farther away.

Hunting as a sport still exists, but many groups campaign against it. Today, few people hunt animals in order to survive. As the world's many vegetarians have proved, it is possible to live without meat.

Perspectives

The International Fund for Animal Welfare campaigns against the seal hunting that takes place in Newfoundland each year. They would like to see the practice banned.

"Seal pups have traditionally been clubbed to death, but in recent years thinning ice has led to increased shooting on ice and in open water. When clubbing, sealers may only 'stun' a pup, resulting in the skinning or bleeding of a live seal. Shooting also causes significant suffering. The Royal Commission on Seals and Sealing recognized it is extremely difficult to guarantee a clean kill when shooting at seals in the water or on moving ice floes. Seals are often wounded and escape to die under the ice."

The International Fund for Animal Welfare web site, July 2003 (www.ifaw.org/ifaw/general/)

Culling or sport?

People have different reasons for hunting animals. Some say they love the thrill of the chase. Others like the skill involved in shooting a moving target. Still others hunt in order to "cull" (reduce the population of a species) the herd.

In the United States, hunting, especially deer hunting, is very popular. Hunters kill deer for their meat, called venison, and their hides, which are made into leather. Deer heads or antlers are often mounted as trophies. Deer hunting is a controversial sport. Deers' natural predators, such as coyotes, wolves, and mountain lions, no longer control the wild deer populations. In the last one hundred years or so, many of these predators were hunted to near extinction themselves—causing deer populations to soar.

Hunters load a gutted deer onto a pickup truck in Texas.

Some deer hunters argue that hunting is humane because, if deer herds were allowed to grow too large, they couldn't find enough food and many deer would starve to death. Others blame deer for destroying farmers' crops. These hunters argue that they help maintain an environmental balance for the deer. Those who hunt other prey, such as pheasants, ducks, geese, quail, fox, rabbit, bear, and mink, claim that hunting prevents their quarry from becoming pests to humans.

Humane alternatives to hunting

Although most animal rights supporters feel that it is wrong to kill animals for sport, or even to cull them, they recognize the overpopulation problem. Humane ways of culling a species include sterilizing animals so that they cannot continue to breed and encouraging birds to lay eggs in artificial nests so that the eggs can easily be removed and destroyed.

A skeet shooter practices his hunting skills by firing at clay pigeons (baked clay or limestone disks). A machine propels the disks into the sky at angles that mimic the flight path of game birds.

"Live traps" catch, rather than kill, mice and other small rodents. These animals are then released unharmed in a different area. Live traps will not decrease the numbers of a species, but will help control a pest problem.

Meanwhile, new humane activities have been developed to take the place of blood sports. With clay-pigeon ("skeet") shooting, a saucer-shaped target of baked clay is fired into the air at different angles. The object of the sport is to shoot at and hit as many clay pigeons as possible.

Perspectives

Support Fox Hunting is a group that is opposed to a proposed ban on hunting foxes with dogs in the United Kingdom:

"Fox hunting with dogs is an age-old sport, a British tradition and a major part of the British countryside. Banning fox hunting will only add to problems in the countryside and will be the start of the end for country sports, with fishing and shooting already under threat."

The Support Fox Hunting web site, June 2003 (www.supportfoxhunting.co.uk/)

Drag hunting is another humane sport that is growing in popularity. Instead of dogs, horses, and riders chasing a wild animal, the hunt follows a trail set by a human. That person leaves a trail by dragging a piece of heavy material soaked with a strong-smelling substance, such as animal dung, through the woods and fields. Hunting dogs pick up the scent and follow the trail. Since a wild animal's primary concern is survival, rather than leaving an exciting trail, drag hunters are almost guaranteed an interesting chase with lots of variety.

Poaching

Laws govern when and where animals can be hunted. People who illegally hunt or catch game or fish on someone else's land or who violate game laws are called poachers. A poacher usually hunts because the animal—or some part of it—can be sold for a large sum of money.

For example, ivory commands a high price on the black market, and African elephants have been poached for their tusks for years. Many laws exist to prevent these illegal killings. Park rangers work hard to protect elephants and other game from poachers. Piano keys and white billiard balls—once made of elephant ivory—are now made from synthetic materials.

The fur debate

Perhaps the most controversial area of hunting concerns the fur industry. When people first hunted, the most important part of an animal was its meat. Its fur was a by-product used to make

Case Study

In Eastern Africa, in May 2002, a female elephant was shot and killed by poachers, but her six-month-old calf escaped. By the time the baby elephant was discovered by a herdsman, it was thirsty, hungry, and very thin. The herdsman arranged for the elephant to be taken to the David Sheldrick Wildlife Trust near Nairobi, Kenya, where it could be nursed back to full health. Named *Mpala*—after the area in which it was found—the elephant is now safe, well, and protected from danger.

The David Sheldrick Wildlife Trust web site (www.sheldrickwildlifetrust.orgl)

SUMMER IS NO HOLIDAY FOR ANIMALS ON FUR FARM

warm clothes. Early North American settlers found a rich supply of pelt animals to support large fur-trading businesses.

Animals such as mink, fox, and chinchilla are now raised on farms in crowded conditions. Meanwhile, trappers still target raccoons, beavers, coyotes, and skunks with leg traps. In the twenty-first century, many animal rights groups have criticized farming, hunting, and trapping of animals for fur. Activists have even splashed blood-red paint on people wearing fur coats to publicize their anti-fur viewpoint.

Protesters at an animal rights demonstration in Helsinki, Finland, cage themselves to raise awareness of the suffering of animals on fur farms.

Debate

Throughout the world's food chain, many animals hunt, kill, and eat other animals. If animals hunt animals, why shouldn't humans hunt animals?

4: ANIMAL RESEARCH

A nimal research takes place for three main reasons: to discover more about animal physiology to help improve the health of both humans and animals; to test medications for animals and humans; and to educate students.

The history of animal research

Animal experiments first took place in ancient Greece over two thousand years ago when scientists cut open live pigs in order to find out how their bodies functioned. Experiments continued through the Middle Ages, with surgeons practicing their skills on animals before performing operations on humans.

By the nineteenth century, animal research had become much more common—and opposition to it increased. Animal research continued its steady growth until the 1950s, which saw a huge increase in the number of experiments on animals for consumer product testing of new drugs, detergents, and cosmetics.

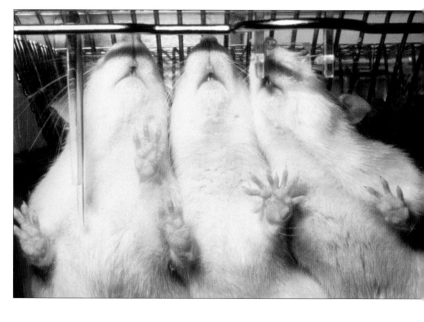

The growing power of the animal rights movement and concerns about animal welfare resulted in greater controls over the use of animals in science. Many countries license animal research laboratories. Some governments also require that animal researchers secure preapproval of the research protocols (procedures and methods) to ensure the safety and well-being of the animals as well as to justify the merits of the experiments.

Millions of animals of many species are still sacrificed in medical and scientific experiments every year. Twenty-first century researchers put a greater emphasis than ever before on alternatives to animal research. Some animal rights and animal welfare groups hope to someday outlaw any animal research in all countries of the world.

Laboratory mice sniff at something held above their cage. Mice are the most common research animals used to test the safety of cosmetics, pesticides, and drugs. Although animal experiments remain controversial and alternatives are being developed, many laws require animal testing before new products are approved for use by humans.

Arguments for and against animal research

Should animals be used in experiments? This question provokes a variety of responses—some positive, some negative, and some extreme. Many people feel that animal research is justified, but only in certain circumstances.

Those who support animal research argue that it is the best way to develop vaccines and medicines for humans. They argue that animals' and humans' bodies are alike in many ways, and that animals suffer from similar illnesses and diseases as humans—which means that humans would probably react in a similar way to a test or drug administered to animals. Also, since animals have shorter life cycles than humans, it takes less time to study them from birth to death.

Humans enjoy enormous medical advances thanks in part to animal research. These include the development of vaccines for diphtheria, measles, polio, smallpox, and tetanus; the use of antibiotics; the regulation of diabetes through insulin use; the determination of chemotherapy dosages; the proper placement of cardiac pacemakers; the discovery of drugs to treat AIDS; and the correct surgical techniques for transplanting organs.

A mother looks on as her son is vaccinated in Nashville, Tennessee. Vaccinations against diseases like smallpox and measles have prevented millions from needless suffering, disability, and death.

Perspectives

Americans for Medical Progress (AMP) favors animal research:

"Virtually all medical advances and discoveries of the [twentieth] century were based in animal research. Examples include vaccines for diseases like smallpox and polio, as well as anesthesia, aspirin and insulin . . . If we were to abolish the use of live animals entirely, we would be unable to investigate how one system (for example, the nervous system) interacts with another (for example, the immune system), while monitoring side effects."

The Americans for Medical Progress web site, June 2003 (www.ampef.orgl)

Those who disagree with animal research argue that animals have the right to live and that humans do not have the right to carry out experiments on them for human needs. Many animal rights supporters believe that humans should be used in experiments instead of animals. Another argument is that animal research results do not necessarily apply to humans. Animal-rights activists may argue that although penicillin acts as an antibiotic to humans, it kills guinea pigs.

There is very strong opposition to experiments performed on animals in order to test nonessential products such as soap, toothpaste, face cream, makeup, and hair spray. Even though many products currently claim no animal testing was conducted, the majority of today's cosmetics contain ingredients that were tested on animals in the past.

Most people find it difficult to decide where they stand on the animal research issue. While many feel that animals should not be used to test cosmetics, they approve of animal research for medical purposes.

Genetic engineering

Each living creature carries genes inside its body that serve as a blueprint for reproduction. For instance, genes passed down from parents determine how offspring will look, form, and behave, and sometimes whether or not they will develop certain diseases during their lifetime. Genetic engineering aims to change living beings—either by altering their genes or by transferring genes from one living being to another.

Worldwide, millions of research animals are genetically modified (undergo genetic engineering) annually for many reasons—some of which are listed below.

Genetic engineering
- enables researchers to increase their knowledge of the functions and reactions of genes
- helps researchers breed farm animals that grow faster or produce more meat, milk, or fur
- reduces animal diseases
- produces animals for use in treating human diseases and animals whose organs are useful for transplanting into humans

Many people who are against genetic engineering believe that humans do not have the right to manipulate animals for their own purposes. They are opposed to any anxiety, suffering, or even death inflicted upon these animals during testing. They also express concern about the possibility of adverse environmental effects of genetically modified animals breeding with wild animals.

Idaho Gem, born in May 2003, is the world's first successfully cloned mule. Scientists in Idaho began the project, which involved complex genetic engineering techniques, in 1998.

Perspectives

"If abandoning animal research means that there are some things we cannot learn, then so be it...We have no basic right...not to be harmed by those natural diseases we are heir to."

Tom Regan, The Case for Animal Rights (Routledge, 1983)

Vivisection

Vivisection is the practice of performing surgical procedures on live animals for the purpose of scientific research. Some people are so against vivisection and other types of animal research that they will do almost anything to prevent these experiments from taking place. Animal liberation groups might stage protests outside research laboratories and even break into the laboratories to free the research animals. Other extreme animal rights supporters resort to violence, such as attacking people who work in stores that sell furs or bombing research facilities, to make their point. These extreme measures of protest are a form of ecoterrorism—the use of radical, often violent, means to protest a perceived threat to the environment or animals. The majority of antivivisectionists, however, rely on peaceful protest to enact change.

An animal rights protester demands an end to animal experimentation at the Huntingdon Life Sciences laboratory near Cambridge, England, in July 2002.

Perspectives

Antivivisection (WA) Inc., in Australia, is against animal research:

"Animal experiments are poorly suited to addressing the urgent health problems of our era, such as…heart disease, cancer, stroke, AIDS and birth defects. The majority of animals in laboratories are used as so-called animal models…researchers try to produce ailments in these animals that 'model' human conditions. The innumerable subtle, but significant, differences between species severely undermines the extrapolation [projection] of animal data to other species, including humans, and delivers often dangerously misleading results."

The Antivivisection (WA) Inc. web site, June 2003 (www.animalliberation.com.au/link/index.htm)

Benefits for animals

Experiments carried out on animals have not just benefited humans—many have helped other animals live longer, healthier lives. Medicines and vaccines developed for use on humans are now also used to treat animals. These include vaccines for rabies and distemper (diseases that

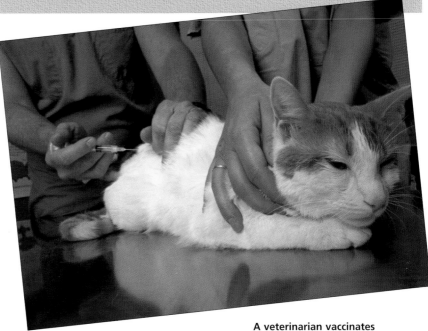

A veterinarian vaccinates a cat against rabies.

Perspectives

"It is not only humans who benefit from medical research: All animals within our care have an interest in it, and the assumption must be that it is so conducted that the long-term benefits to all of us, human and animal, outweigh the short-term costs in pain and discomfort."

Roger Scruton, Animal Rights and Wrongs *(Metro Books, 2000)*

affect dogs and other animals) and treatment to prevent tuberculosis in cattle. Animal research supporters also claim that information learned from such experiments has helped solve many breeding, feeding, and pollution problems faced by wild animals or endangered species in a changing environment.

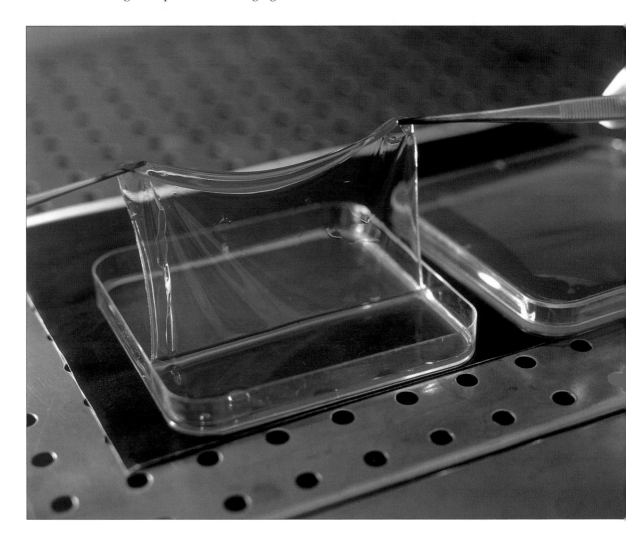

Alternatives to animal research

In 1959, British researchers William Russell and Rex Burch introduced three ways of reducing or preventing animal suffering, known as "the three Rs"—replacement, reduction, and refinement.

Replacement involves substituting animal experiments with tests on cells or tissues grown in laboratories. Corrositex is one type of artificial skin that can substitute for living animal or human skin in experiments.

Laboratories can produce synthetic (artificial) skin for use as skin grafts for patients with serious burns or other injuries. Synthetic skin can also substitute for using research animals in tests of chemical reactions on skin.

Case Study

In 1927, researchers developed a toxicity experiment to measure the poison levels of chemical exposures and drug doses. Called the "Lethal-Dose 50," or "LD$_{50}$ test," the experimental procedure means that a single dose of a drug or chemical at that concentration caused the death of half of the animals on which it was tested. Animal rights supporters around the world condemned LD$_{50}$ experiments because of the enormous suffering caused to animals. Others questioned whether LD$_{50}$ test were even accurate, since the same laboratory often achieved different results when identical tests were repeated. In December 2002, as a result of continued protests, the LD$_{50}$ test was banned by the Organization for Economic Cooperation and Development (OECD), an international organization that oversees testing guidelines for experiments.

Medical and veterinary colleges increasingly use interactive computer programs and videos to demonstrate dissection and other veterinary techniques, thus replacing actual animals.

Reduction means reducing the number of animals used in a particular experiment. Computer programs capable of in-depth analysis now evaluate research data. This means that fewer tests are necessary to get results. Also, researchers studying different aspects of anatomy or physiology may perform several experiments on the same animal instead of sacrificing another.

Finally, refinement means altering experiments to lessen the suffering of the animals involved. More effective use of painkillers, improved living conditions, and better handling techniques all help. Ultrasound scanning, which uses sound waves to study organs inside an animal without cutting it open, offers researchers yet another option. Perhaps the best type of refinement is a research design that does not cause the death of the animal.

Debate

Many small mammals, such as rats, mice, rabbits, and guinea pigs, are bred specifically for animal research. Is human benefit more important than the suffering these animals may undergo? Where should animal researchers draw the line?

5: PETS

Pet owners face a huge responsibility. All pets have different needs. For instance, dogs need daily walks, cats need access to a litter box, and rabbits need the company of other rabbits.

The history of pets

People keep animals as pets to enjoy their company and companionship. Many of the most popular pets, such as cats and dogs, are domesticated—that is, they are tame and trained to behave in a particular way. In contrast, instinct and survival dictates the lifestyle and behavior patterns of wild animals.

The first domesticated animal was most likely a dog tamed thousands of years ago. Ancient Egyptians pampered small dogs, and greyhounds hunted with their owners. Egyptians also tamed lions, hyenas, and monkeys. Cats, however, proved the most popular pet of the time. Ancient Egyptians considered cats sacred and worshiped them in temples.

Throughout history, people have used pets to help with hunting, guarding or herding other animals, protecting

A hamster makes a good pet for apartment dwellers. Hamsters require less care than dogs and cats.

Perspectives

Brian Kilcommons is an experienced dog owner and trainer:
"With their unquestioning devotion comes obligation. Caring for a dog is a commitment...We owe them our highest selves, not our...anger or impatience. Why a dog? In short, to love and be loved."

Brian Kilcommons and Sarah Wilson, Good Owners, Great Dogs *(Warner Books, 1999)*

Case Study

Every year, animal shelters all over the world help millions of animals that are neglected, abused, or unwanted. Peanut (below), a Jack Russell terrier, was rescued in the United Kingdom by the Royal Society for the Prevention of Cruelty to Animals (RSPCA).

Peanut was only eight months old when an RSPCA inspector found him cowering in a ferret cage, covered with fleas and sores. He was suffering from mange (sore, ulcerated skin) and significant hair loss. He also had overgrown claws. As the RSPCA inspector attempted to take Peanut away, the dog's owner stopped her. He offered to shoot Peanut to put him out of his misery. The inspector declined this offer and instead took Peanut to a shelter.

In August 2002, a court found Peanut's owner guilty of causing unnecessary suffering to the dog by failing to get veterinary treatment. Although he was not jailed, the man was fined.

Fortunately, Peanut made a full recovery and found a loving new home. His was just one of many stories highlighted by the RSPCA in their 2002 campaign against cruelty to animals.

Peanut is one of the success stories of a pet rescued from a shelter.

property owners, or catching mice, rats, and other pests. Pets are now at the center of a huge industry that not only sells a variety of animals but also offers services, such as pet health care, training, and grooming.

The pet food and accessories market employs millions of people worldwide. Some people earn extra money as pet sitters when the owner is on vacation. Others specialize in exercising the pets of owners who are too busy to walk them regularly. Pet cemeteries offer owners a permanent resting spot for their beloved companions. Finally, and most importantly, animal welfare organizations ensure that animals are well treated.

A new pet

Pets can be bought from pet shops or breeders, adopted from rescue centers, or (in the case of goldfish) sometimes won as prizes at fairs—which can raise protests from animal-rights activists.

Pet breeders rear and sell certain "purebred" animals, such as poodles or Siamese cats. Some people insist on owning a pet purchased from a breeding establishment.

Unwanted, neglected, or stray pets, including dogs, cats, hamsters, rabbits, and even horses, might wind up at a rescue shelter. If they're healthy and lucky, new owners will adopt them. Most shelters ask potential pet owners a series of questions regarding the animal they wish to adopt, such as:

Plastic bags filled with goldfish hang at an outdoor market in Jakarta, Indonesia.

• Why do you want an animal?
• Where will the animal be kept?
• Is your house suitable?
• What other animals live in the house?
• Will the animal be left alone at any time during the day?

Rescue shelters use the answers to determine whether or not the people and pets are a good match and to ensure that the home is suitable. For example, some animals, such as large dogs, need lots of room to move around outdoors, so a high-rise apartment is not a good place for them to live.

Perspectives

The Center for Animal Care and Control (CACC) is a nonprofit organization that rescues, shelters, and places homeless and abandoned animals in New York City:

"...we feel strongly that shelters are the best source for acquiring a pet. CACC evaluates all animals entering the system for both health and temperament. We...make informed decisions about the appropriateness of an animal for specific circumstances. These may include homes with young children or other pets, or families who are away from the home for long hours each day. The CACC adoption staff cares deeply about the success of the placement, not the monetary value of a sale."

The New York Center for Animal Care and Control web site (www.nycacc.org/)

Unfortunately, hundreds of thousands of animals are put to death every year because no one wants to adopt them. Animal welfare supporters suggest that pet lovers buy pets from a rescue shelter rather than a pet breeder or a pet shop. With so many homeless animals in the world, they feel that it is important to give these unwanted pets a home, instead of encouraging the breeding of even more animals.

Exotic pets

Cats, dogs, hamsters, and gerbils have been domesticated so that they are suited to life with humans. Some people also keep exotic animals, such as monkeys, snakes, and iguanas, as pets.

Many people believe that it is wrong to remove wild animals from their natural environment to keep as pets. Also, because few people truly understand and can provide for the needs of orangutans, tigers, or alligators, it often poses serious problems for owners. For instance, owners of exotic pets may be unable to afford to duplicate the habitat of their pet's natural environment.

A puppy waits for a new owner at a pet shelter.

Perspectives

People for the Ethical Treatment of Animals (PETA) is a worldwide animal rights organization:

"In a perfect world, animals would be free...However, domesticated dogs and cats cannot survive 'free' in our concrete jungles, so we must take as good care of them as possible. People with the time, money, love, and patience to make a lifetime commitment to an animal can make an enormous difference by adopting from shelters or rescuing animals from a perilous life on the street. But it is also important to stop manufacturing 'pets,' thereby perpetuating [continuing to breed] a class of animals forced to rely on humans to survive."

PETA pamphlet, "Companion Animals: Pets or Prisoners?"

Campaigns by organizations such as the World Wildlife Fund in the United States and Canada (known as WWF internationally) have helped enact laws banning the sale of wild animals in some countries.

Selective breeding

Selective breeding is the process of mating animals with prized characteristics, such as height, weight, or a certain kind of fur, to produce offspring that are likely to exhibit many of the same characteristics as the parent animals. Humans have practiced selective breeding of animals for thousands of years.

Selective breeding has also created many different types of animals. For instance, greyhounds

A woman in Moscow, Russia, feeds her pet cobra. Exotic pets have become fashionable in Russia.

were bred for their long and sleek bodies to serve as race dogs, while short, stocky terriers were bred for their ability to chase prey into small burrows and dens. Hundreds of years ago, bulldogs were bred to irritate bulls in bull-baiting competitions.

Selective breeding programs have caused may health problems for these animals. For example, a bulldog's lower jawbone is longer than its upper jawbone. This enables the dog to hold its grip when biting—but the shape of its head and nostrils means that bulldogs have breathing difficulties. So while selective breeding can produce an animal that benefits humans, the practice does not necessarily benefit the animals.

A Beijing, China, cat owner shows off her white cat with one yellow eye and one blue eye. In China, the different-colored eyes are highly prized, but if the selective breeding used to achieve the odd eye colors results instead in two blue eyes, the white cat is often deaf.

Debate

Is it fair to animals to keep them as pets? What about domestic animals that have been bred to make good companions? Should these be returned to the wild? Would they be able to survive?

6: ANIMAL ENTERTAINMENT

Should animals perform in order to entertain humans? Is it fair to make dolphins jump through hoops to please a crowd? Are zoos justified? Many people feel that the answer to all of these questions is "No." Other people enjoy watching dolphin shows and visiting zoos. Who is right?

The history of animal entertainment

People have used animals for entertainment for thousands of years. The Romans captured wild animals in North Africa, shipped them to Rome, and made them fight each other to death in front of crowds at the Colosseum. Later, in Britain, from the Middle Ages onward, large audiences gathered to watch bear-baiting contests, where a chained bear would be attacked and tormented by fierce dogs.

Blood sports involve hunting, wounding, or killing animals. Cockfighting (pitting birds, such as roosters, against each other) and dogfighting were once very popular events. Cheering crowds, who bet large sums of money on the outcome of the

A fourteenth-century illustration from the Luttrell Psalter (a special book containing prayers and an illustrated history of the times) shows dogs tormenting a chained bear.

Perspectives

The first dolphin show took place in Florida in 1938:

"The dolphin show does represent a form of education but it's a form of bad education in that it teaches millions of people that human supremacy over nature is a good thing."

Helene O'Barry, The Dolphin Project web site (www.dolphinproject.org/)

fights would watch these cruel "sports," which usually ended with the death of one animal. While most countries ban cockfighting and dogfighting, illegal fights still occur.

Many people enjoy watching other types of sports or entertainment involving animals, including bullfighting, horse racing, and dog racing. All continue to arouse fierce debate.

Bullfighting

Bullfighting has been popular in Spain, Portugal, and parts of southern France and Latin America since the early sixteenth century. Bulls bred to be savage and strong are released into a bullring to face a matador (the bullfighter). Tens of thousands of bulls are killed in bullfights every year, and their deaths are rarely quick. In the bullring, the bulls may be harpooned and tortured with flames, spears, and swords. This treatment enrages animal-rights supporters around the world.

Case Study

In the nineteenth and twentieth centuries, wild capuchin monkeys were tamed, then forced to walk upright and trained to work for organ-grinders. While the street musician worked the barrel organ, the monkey collected money from onlookers.

In May 2001, the Jungle Friends Primate Sanctuary in Gainesville, Florida, rescued Jimmy, a forty-year-old capuchin monkey. He had suffered years of abuse at the hands of an organ-grinder before being sold to a pet shop, where he was used to attract customers. Jimmy will now spend the rest of his life at the sanctuary with Chi Chi, a former circus monkey.

The Jungle Friends web site, June 2003 (www.junglefriends.orglindex.shtml)

Perspectives

The *Time Out* guide to the Andalucía region of Spain describes the end of a bullfight:

"If the matador is accurate and swift, there is little blood; the animal pauses and there is total silence in the ring; it sways slightly, staggers, its front legs give way and it collapses. However, if the kill is not clean, things can get very messy indeed; the bull will start staggering around, glassy-eyed, throwing up gallons of blood…while the matador either tries to finish the job himself with a…sword or instructs one of his men to stab the bull in the brain with a tiny dagger. Either way, it's horribly distressing to watch."

Time Out: Andalucía *(Penguin, 2002)*

At the end of the twentieth century, two hundred thousand people—more than 1 percent of the Spanish workforce—were employed in the bullfighting industry. Those who approve of bullfighting argue that they would lose jobs if the practice were banned. While there are no signs of a total ban in the near future, animal activists have made some progress. The Spanish towns of Tossa de Mar, Vilamcolum, and La Varjol have banned bullfighting, and Jalapa, Mexico, has also outlawed the "sport."

A matador teases a bull with his cape during a bullfight in the Camargue region of France.

Circuses

Wild animals were first used in a circus performance in 1831. Since then, circuses have used lions, snakes, tigers, polar bears, giraffes, hippos, rhinos, and elephants in their acts.

Animal rights and welfare supporters argue that circuses often remove wild animals from their natural habitat and that it degrades the dignity of the animals to use them to entertain humans with tricks. Reports of animal abuse, such as beating chimpanzees or using whips and electric prods to force elephants and other wild animals to perform their stunts, occasionally occur.

Since the 1970s, many circuses have reduced the use of animals in their acts. An increasing number of circuses are also working toward featuring only human performers. Animal rights workers hope to completely eliminate the use of animal acts. That way, circus audiences can continue to enjoy all the fun of the big top without involving any animals in the performances.

Indian elephants perform in the Moscow State Circus in Russia.

Perspectives

The Society for the Prevention of Cruelty to Animals in British Columbia, Canada, is working to ban the use of circus animals around the world:

"Most of a circus animal's life is spent travelling in cramped trucks . . . The only freedom and exercise they receive is while performing. Former animal trainers report observing or participating in abusive training practices such as beating or electroshocking bears, elephants, big cats, and chimpanzees to force them to perform tricks. This is the price circus animals pay so that the public can have a few laughs."

The British Columbia Society for the Prevention of Cruelty to Animals web site (www.spca.bc.ca/animalsense/Fall2000/CircusFall2000.htm)

Perspectives

In part of California's 1,800-acre (728-hectare) San Diego Wild Animal Park, the animals roam freely and the people are contained! Visitors view herds of animals native to Africa and Eurasia from aboard an electric monorail train that travels the grounds. The Park also includes a North American exhibit, endangered animals, and "indicator species" that indicate the health of the surroundings:

"By monitoring them, we can assess the status of the ecosystem in which they live," says Michael Mace, curator (of birds).

www.sandiegozoo.org/wap/visitor_info.html

Zoos

Zoos exist for a number of reasons: to display wild animals to people who might otherwise never see such animals; to study the animals and their behavior; to educate people, to help conserve rare species; and to make money.

A hippopotamus rests in its enclosure at the government-run zoo in Santiago, Chile. Cramped enclosures and deteriorating conditions focused worldwide attention on efforts to build a new, privately run zoo.

Opponents object to zoos because the animals often live in spaces that are nothing like their natural habitat. In the last century, animals were often kept behind bars or in concrete enclosures. Conditions are improving. Modern zoos attempt to imitate the conditions of an animal's home—although the expenses involved make it very difficult for smaller zoos to feature such areas. The biggest zoos allow plenty of room for animals to roam. Safari parks that allow animals to live in environments that are most like the wild are becoming increasingly popular. Visitors view animals from aboard trains or special cars that travel through the zoo grounds.

Some zoo animals have been captured from the wild, while others have been born in captivity. The capturing of animals from their natural habitat often breaks up the social order of the animal groups. Animal-rights supporters feel that either way of restocking zoos is wrong.

Proponents of zoos argue that they allow scientists to observe and study wild animals. Zoos allow endangered species to breed safely in captivity. Finally, zoos mean that people can see animals from all over the world—no matter where they live.

People who are against zoos feel that even these reasons do not justify keeping wild animals in captivity.

Horses

The majority of the world's horses are domesticated, which means they are kept as pets, as working animals for police departments and on farms, or as show or sporting animals. Horses may participate in jumping competitions, racing, pony-and-trap racing, and rodeos. In each of these events, the horses obey the commands of a human trainer or jockey.

Some types of horse racing can be extremely dangerous for both horse and rider. Sometimes the horses collide and are horribly injured or even die during the competitions. Horse lovers and animal lovers worldwide have called for a ban on horse racing. They feel that horses should not be forced to participate in activities that could lead to injury or death.

Horses vault an obstacle during a steeplechase race in Saratoga Springs, New York.

Debate

Are some forms of animal entertainment less harmful to animals than others, or should they all be banned?

7: ENDANGERED SPECIES

In the twenty-first century, hunting, loss of habitat, pollution, and the introduction of non-native animals threaten the survival of thousands of wild animal species. Do animals have the right to be protected even if doing so is expensive and causes inconveniences for humans?

Humans and non-native animals introduced by humans caused the extinction of dodo birds in the seventeenth century.

Hunted to extinction

During the last two thousand years, human actions have directly or indirectly led to the extinction of a number of animal species, such as the dodo bird, the passenger pigeon, and the Carolina parakeet. Portuguese settlers helped cause the extinction of the dodo, a flightless bird that lived on Mauritius (an island off Africa in the Indian Ocean), within two hundred years of their arrival. No animal welfare organizations existed at the time to protect

Perspectives

The director of the International Gorilla Conservation Program (IGCP), is pleased that numbers of endangered mountain gorillas in Uganda, Rwanda, and the Democratic Republic of Congo have increased since 1989. Threats to the apes include hunting, capture for the illegal pet trade, and habitat loss caused by a local war:

"International and national efforts to protect this species have pulled the mountain gorilla back from the brink of extinction. If we want to ensure that they survive another hundred years, we must ensure that we lift the pressures that still threaten their forest home," says Dr. Annette Lanjouw.

The BBC news web site, June 2003 (http://news.bbc.co.uk/)

native species from human hunting or from animals introduced by humans into a new environment. The dodos showed no fear of the newcomers and had no way to defend themselves from their new predators. They were all easily killed by humans and the non-native ("exotic") animals, such as pigs and rats.

Now, international laws aim to protect animals from extinction. The 1977 Convention on International Trade in Endangered Species (CITES) banned the selling of products from endangered animals. Unfortunately, poaching—illegal hunting and killing—of many species still occurs. For example, since 1970, the world's rhinoceros population declined by 90 percent, mostly because a rhino's horn is worth thousands of dollars in some countries.

In other types of hunting, the animal is killed simply so the hunter can mount and display its head, skin, or other parts as a trophy. Animals are also taken from the wild to make fur coats or to live as exotic pets or in zoos. Animal supporters believe that humans do not have the right to remove an animal from its natural home, wear its fur, or waste an animal for show.

Some cultures believe that eating or wearing certain animal parts, such as antlers, ears, horns, hooves, or front paws of a variety of rare animals holds special healing powers or energies. The prominent nasal horn of Africa's black rhinoceros makes it a favorite target of poachers, who usually leave the rest of the body to rot. Millions of rhinoceros once roamed Africa and Asia; now only about ten thousand exist. Poaching has also caused a huge drop in populations of other wild animals around the globe.

Shrinking animal habitats

The habitats of many species, such as lions, elephants, pandas, and chimpanzees, shrink annually as people develop wild areas to accommodate the world's increasing human population. Crops cover large spreads, while towns spring up in the middle of nowhere. New roads fragment animal territories, making it difficult for wild species to find mates.

In some developing countries, well-managed wildlife reserves offer the best hope of survival for wild animals, but native peoples may argue that they have a right to live off the same land and use the animals as needed.

Pollution

Any environmental change affects the health and welfare of wild animals. Air, water, and soil pollution is disastrous for the habitats and lifestyles of native animal species. Sometimes what is good for humans

The *Exxon Valdez* (on left) caused a huge oil spill that devastated wildlife on the Alaskan coast in March 1989.

Case Study

The Orangutan Foundation International (OFI) is dedicated to the conservation of wild orangutans and their rain forest habitat in Indonesia and Malaysia.

In 1999, a young female orangutan was orphaned and made homeless by palm-oil plantation developers. Local villagers captured the orangutan and tied her up with wire cables. They were about to kill her and sell her body parts to developers who hoped to rid the area of this endangered species when a passing truck driver saw what was happening and contacted OFI.

The young orangutan was rescued by OFI and taken to one of their care centers. They named her "Ingrid." When she had recovered from her ordeal, Ingrid was returned to the wild.

The Orangutan Foundation International web site, June 2003 (www.orangutan.org/home/home.php)

proves a bad thing for animals. For instance, pesticides and fertilizers not only affect pests, but also damage valued species. Queen conch (pronounced "konk") are a variety of snail native to the Florida Keys. Conch grow very large and produce a heavy shell with a pink lining. Conch meat is used in many dishes and the shells are made into jewelry or put on display. These animals were once so common that people who were born and grew up in the Keys are known as "Conchs." While pesticide spraying helps control the mosquito population in the Keys, bolsters the local economy, and encourages tourism, it also is one of the factors causing a dramatic decrease in the numbers of Queen Conch larvae that survive to adulthood. Animal rights groups may protest that this situation is not a fair trade for the snails.

Humans also cause environmental disasters. In 1989, the *Exxon Valdez* oil spill in Prince William Sound ruined about 1,500 miles

(2,400 kilometers) of Alaskan coastline and killed or sickened millions of fish, birds, and sea mammals.

The burning of fossil fuels, such as oil and coal, releases carbon dioxide and other gases into the air, creating a "greenhouse effect" that traps solar heat energy in Earth's atmosphere and raises worldwide temperatures. Penguins are among the species whose territory is shrinking as the Antarctic ice melts. Some say that humans have a moral obligation to prevent pollution.

Thanks in part to global warming, glaciers around the world are melting at alarming rates. This glacier in Qaanaaq, Greenland, is receding at a record pace.

Non-native animals

Imported, "exotic" creatures often have a harmful effect on a new environment. Animal protection groups fight to protect native animal species by working to enforce practices that prohibit the deliberate or accidental transfer of animals from one area of the planet to another.

For instance, when people brought rabbits to Australia in the late nineteenth century, no one realized the problems they would

Giant pandas Mei Xiang and Tian Tian, on loan from the China Research and Conservation Center, feed on bamboo, their favorite food, at the Smithsonian National Zoological Park (commonly called the National Zoo) in Washington, D.C., in 2002.

Perspectives

In 1998, the Pennsylvania Twenty-First Century Environment Commission released its report on conserving natural resources:

"Plants, animals, fungi and micro-organisms . . . in combination weave the web that holds together . . . all life on Earth. The quality and strength of the web is dependent on the quality of our natural support systems—water, land, and air . . . The diversity of life is a key measure of the health of our environment now and of its future reliability . . . for humans."

The Pennsylvania Twenty-First Century Environment Commission web site (www.21stcentury.state.pa.us)

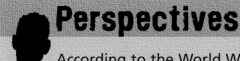

Perspectives

According to the World Wildlife Fund (WWF):

"The need to reduce and repair habitat loss, to cut down on our reliance on persistent chemicals, to combat global warming, prevent the introduction of alien species, stop the illegal trade in animal parts...it is all within our power to stop and reverse the destructive trends that we see. From what we buy in the shops, to what we say and read, who[m] we vote for, and what we campaign for—this is where the pressure must come from if governments, business, and industry are to make the changes that will ultimately conserve life on Earth."

The World Wildlife Fund web site (www.worldwildlife.org)

cause. The rabbits escaped into the wild, bred like crazy, and soon covered the entire continent, grazing in areas where native animals lived and leaving little food for the Australian wildlife. In the 1950s, a plan to control the rabbit population by purposely spreading a deadly rabbit disease failed. Animal welfare groups hope to prevent a similar situation from occurring again.

Helping animals survive
Animal supporters believe that humans have a responsibility to save endangered species from extinction by
- educating people about the relationship between their standard of living and its effect on local and global animal environments
- working with governments and local communities to develop strategies for dealing with these problems
- creating public awareness about habitat destruction and environmental problems

No matter which side people may take—that it is acceptable for humans to use animals and their products, or that no species has the right to exploit another—animals deserve protection from abuse and preservation of their natural dignity.

Debate

How should humans decide which species to preserve? Is it more important to protect cute, cuddly mammals than slimy snakes? Should saving the pandas receive more funding and publicity than saving snails?

GLOSSARY

activist a person who campaigns vigorously for a cause to bring about change.

anesthesia drugs or gases used to help patients from feeling pain during a procedure.

antibiotic medicine that kills microorganisms.

by-product a different object made from what is left after the original product is created.

cloning creating genetically identical cells, animals, or plants.

conservation preserving or restoring the environment and wildlife.

crustacea creatures with a hard outer skeleton, such as crabs, lobsters, and shrimps.

diphtheria a deadly disease that causes swelling of the throat.

dissection cutting up a body or a plant in order to study it.

distemper a disease that causes fever and coughing in animals.

ecosystem all the plants and animals in a particular environment, such as a pond, a forest, or a cave.

electroshocking the practice of using a jolt of electricity in order to control or enforce an animal's behavior or movement.

exotic animals or plants that are introduced to a new, non-native geographical location.

exploitation to use a resource for the benefit of one species at the expense of another.

extinction the death of every animal or plant of a particular species.

fertilizer waste matter or chemicals applied to soil and crops to make plants grow at a faster rate.

free-range a farming method for animals (usually poultry) that allows them to move about freely while foraging (finding food).

gene a tiny section of biologic material passed from a parent organism to its offspring that contains the code for forming certain traits, such as hair length or eye color.

habitat the environment in which humans, animals, or plants live.

humane a type of treatment toward animals or humans that is as gentle, compassionate, and painless as possible.

immune system the tissues and cells that defend the body against infection.

microorganisms very small living things, such as bacteria, viruses, or fungi.

organic grown without chemicals.

pesticide a chemical used to kill or control animal or plant pests.

polio (poliomyelitis) a viral disease that affects nerve and muscle control and can cause permanent paralysis.

quarry a prey animal.

rennet a product from the stomach of a calf that helps curdle milk to produce cheese.

smallpox a deadly viral disease that causes fever and skin blisters.

species a group of creatures that displays common features, such as stripes or horns, by which they are identified.

tetanus ("lockjaw") a disease caused from the toxic by-product of a bacterium that enters the body through a wound. Tetanus causes muscles spasms and rigidity.

tuberculosis ("TB") an infectious disease of humans and some animals that usually causes growths in the lungs but can infect other body organs as well.

vaccine a medicine that helps prevent disease.

vivisection the practice of performing operations on live animals for research.

BOOKS

Catalano, Julie and Russell E. Train. *Animal Welfare. Earth at Risk* (series).
Raintree/Steck Vaughn, 1994.

Gellatley, Juliet. *The Livewire Guide to Going, Being and Staying Veggie!*
Livewire Books for Teenagers, 1997.

Green, Alan. *Animal Underworld: Inside America's Black Market for Rare and Exotic Species.*
Center for Public Integrity, 1999.

James, Barbara. *Talking Points: Animal Rights.* Raintree/Steck Vaughn, 1999.

Miller-Schroeder, Patricia. *The ASPCA. International Organizations* (series). Weigl Educational, 2003.

Rochford, Deirdre. *Rights for Animals? Viewpoints* (series). Franklin Watts, 1997.

Scruton, Roger. *Animal Rights and Wrongs.* 3rd ed. Claridge Press, 2003.

WEB SITES

www.aspca.org
Visit the ASPCA (American Society for the Prevention of Cruelty to Animals)
web site for the latest news on its activities.

www.ciwf.co.uk
Learn about the Compassion in World Farming's efforts against factory farms.

www.fawc.org.uk/freedoms.htm
Read about the "Five Freedoms" for acceptable animal welfare as established
by the United Kingdom's Farm Animal Welfare Council.

www.friendsofanimals.org
Follow various links to a variety of causes supported by the Friends of Animals.

www.petakids.com/index.html
View "The Meatrix" to learn more about the treatment of farm animals
and find out how kids can help make changes.

www.wwf.org/
Discover the habitats and behaviors of many different wild animals from
the global environmental network of the World Wildlife Fund.

INDEX

Numbers in **bold** refer to images.